PLANET EARTH

THE WATER CYCLE

ABDO
Publishing Company

Big
Buddy BOOKS
Planet Earth

Marcia Zappa

VISIT US AT
www.abdopublishing.com

Published by ABDO Publishing Company, 8000 West 78th Street, Edina, Minnesota 55439.

Printed in the United States of America, North Mankato, Minnesota.
032010
092010

 PRINTED ON RECYCLED PAPER

Coordinating Series Editor: Rochelle Baltzer
Contributing Editors: Heidi M.D. Elston, Megan M. Gunderson, BreAnn Rumsch, Sarah Tieck
Graphic Design: Adam Craven
Cover Photograph: *Shutterstock*: Leksele.
Interior Photographs/Illustrations: *AP Photo*: Russel A. Daniels, File (p. 13), Misha Japaridze, File (p. 11);
    Corbis: ©Fred Hirschmann/Science Faction (p. 15); *iStockphoto*: ©iStockphoto.com/blackestockphoto
    (p. 21), ©iStockphoto.com/Blue-Cutler (p. 27), ©iStockphoto.com/slobo (p. 27); NASA (p. 5); *Peter
    Arnold, Inc.*: ©Biosphoto/Frank Fouquet (p. 25), Jacques Jangoux (p. 23), Steven Kaufman (p. 5), Jim
    Wark (p. 5); *Photo Researchers, Inc.*: ©M-Sat Ltd (p. 11); *Shutterstock*: CAN BALCIOGLU (p. 7),
    Ramunas Bruzas (p. 30), Magdalena Bujak (p. 19), Matthew Cole (p. 9), Stephen Denness (p. 7),Tischenko
    Irina (p. 7), kwestt (p. 5), Chee-Onn Leong (p. 17), Sean Nel (p. 29), Tatiana Popova (p. 17), Serg64
    (p. 19), Serp (p. 15), Smit (p. 21).

Library of Congress Cataloging-in-Publication Data

Zappa, Marcia, 1985-
 The water cycle / Marcia Zappa.
    p. cm. -- (Planet Earth)
 ISBN 978-1-61613-495-2
 1. Hydrologic cycle--Juvenile literature. I. Title.
 GB848.Z37 2010
 551.48--dc22
                          2009053342

TABLE OF CONTENTS

Water World 4

Solid, Liquid, and Gas 6

Around It Goes 8

On the Surface 10

Deep Below the Ground 12

Evaporation 14

Condensation 18

Drip Drop 22

Water Supply 26

Down to Earth 30

Important Words 31

Web Sites 31

Index 32

WATER WORLD

Water is an important part of planet Earth. It covers about 70 percent of Earth's surface. It is necessary for the survival of all living things.

Earth's water is constantly changing. It moves from oceans to air to land and back. This pattern is known as the water cycle. It has existed for billions of years. Life on Earth depends on it!

The amount of water on Earth never changes. There is the same amount today as when dinosaurs lived!

SOLID, LIQUID, AND GAS

In the water cycle, water exists in three forms. It can be a solid, a liquid, or a gas. In solid form, it is snow or ice. In liquid form, it is water. And in gas form, it is water vapor.

People often use ice to keep their drinks cool.

All living things need water to survive.

Steam from a tea kettle is a form of water vapor.

AROUND IT GOES

The water cycle describes how water changes and moves. The cycle has no beginning or end. Water can stop, skip a step, or even go backward through the cycle.

There are three basic steps in the water cycle. These are evaporation, condensation, and precipitation.

THE WATER CYCLE

CONDENSATION

CLOUD

RAIN

WATER VAPOR

PRECIPITATION

ICE AND SNOW

EVAPORATION

RIVER

OCEAN

ON THE SURFACE

There are two kinds of water in the water cycle. They are salt water and freshwater. Both can be found on Earth's surface.

Oceans consist of salt water. Rivers, streams, and lakes usually consist of freshwater. Rain and snow feed all bodies of water. Some rivers, streams, and lakes feed oceans.

Lake Baikal (*right*) is a large lake in Asia. It contains 20 percent of Earth's unfrozen freshwater! Another 20 percent is in the Great Lakes (*left*) in the United States.

THE GREAT LAKES

DEEP BELOW THE GROUND

Water exists below Earth's surface, too. It **seeps** down through holes and cracks in rocks and soil. This **process** is called infiltration.

Plants soak up some of this water to grow. Other water moves through rocks and soil to feed bodies of water.

The rest of the water travels deep underground. It is stored in rock **formations** called aquifers. It can stay there for a long time.

Water can be pumped out of aquifers through wells. Aquifers are important sources of freshwater for people all over the world.

EVAPORATION

The sun heats water on Earth's surface. This causes the water to change from a liquid into a gas. This **process** is called evaporation. When water evaporates, it becomes water vapor. In this form, it moves from Earth's surface into the **atmosphere**.

About 85 percent of the water in Earth's atmosphere evaporated from oceans.

SCIENCE SPOT

Ice and snow can turn into a gas without ever melting. This process is called sublimation.

Water vapor is always in the air. It is in drops too small for the human eye to see. The word *humidity* describes the amount of water vapor in the air.

Wet places, such as beaches (*left*), tend to have more water vapor. Dry places, such as deserts (*below*), have less water vapor.

CONDENSATION

As water vapor rises in the **atmosphere**, it cools. This causes it to change back into a liquid. This **process** is called condensation.

When water vapor condenses, it forms water drops. High in the atmosphere, billions of drops join together to make a cloud.

In hot weather, condensation forms water drops on the outside of a cold drink.

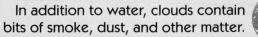 In addition to water, clouds contain bits of smoke, dust, and other matter.

Condensation also forms fog and dew. Fog is similar to clouds, but it forms near Earth's surface.

Dew forms when water vapor condenses on objects near the ground. These water drops often appear on grass and leaves in the early morning.

Fog makes it difficult to see far distances.

Dew forms more easily when there is much water vapor in the air. Calm, clear nights also help dew form.

DRIP DROP

Inside a cloud, water drops grow. When they become heavy enough, they fall to Earth. This **process** is known as precipitation.

Most precipitation falls as rain. But in cold air, water drops can freeze. They fall as hail, sleet, or snow.

Precipitation supplies land with freshwater.

When precipitation falls, the water cycle continues. Much rain and snow falls into oceans. The rest falls on land and into rivers, streams, and lakes.

Some precipitation that falls on land evaporates right back into the air. The rest runs into bodies of water or **seeps** into the ground.

Precipitation can evaporate even before it hits land. Some raindrops turn back into vapor as they fall to Earth.

WATER SUPPLY

Even though most of Earth is covered with water, very little of it is usable. Only 3 percent of Earth's water is fresh. And, much freshwater is deep underground in aquifers or frozen in **glaciers**.

Water is important for all life on Earth. People use a lot of freshwater in their daily lives. If it is not used carefully, **shortages** can occur.

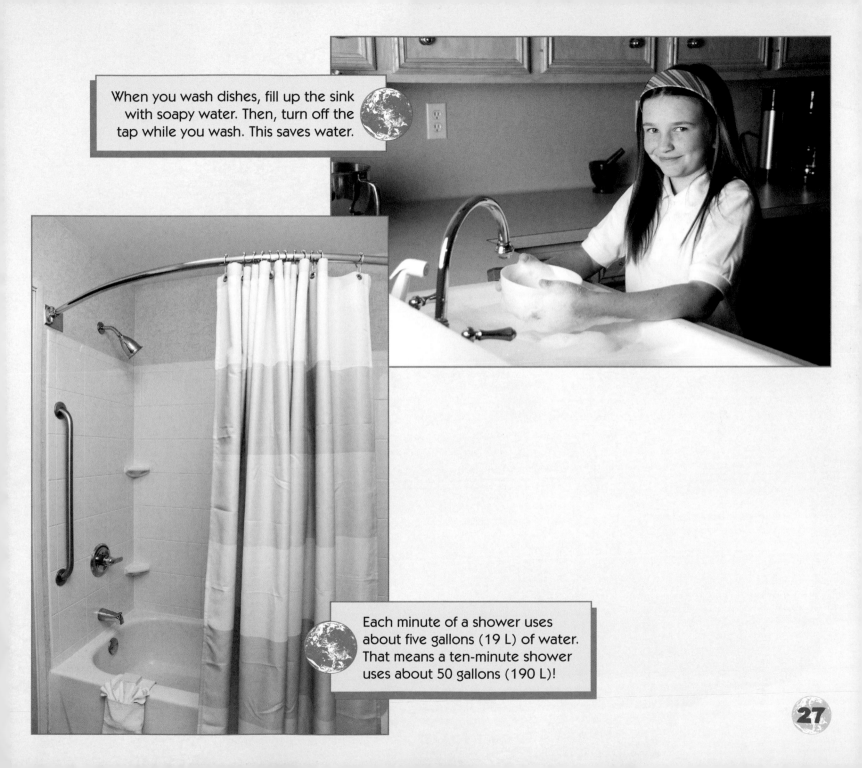

When you wash dishes, fill up the sink with soapy water. Then, turn off the tap while you wash. This saves water.

Each minute of a shower uses about five gallons (19 L) of water. That means a ten-minute shower uses about 50 gallons (190 L)!

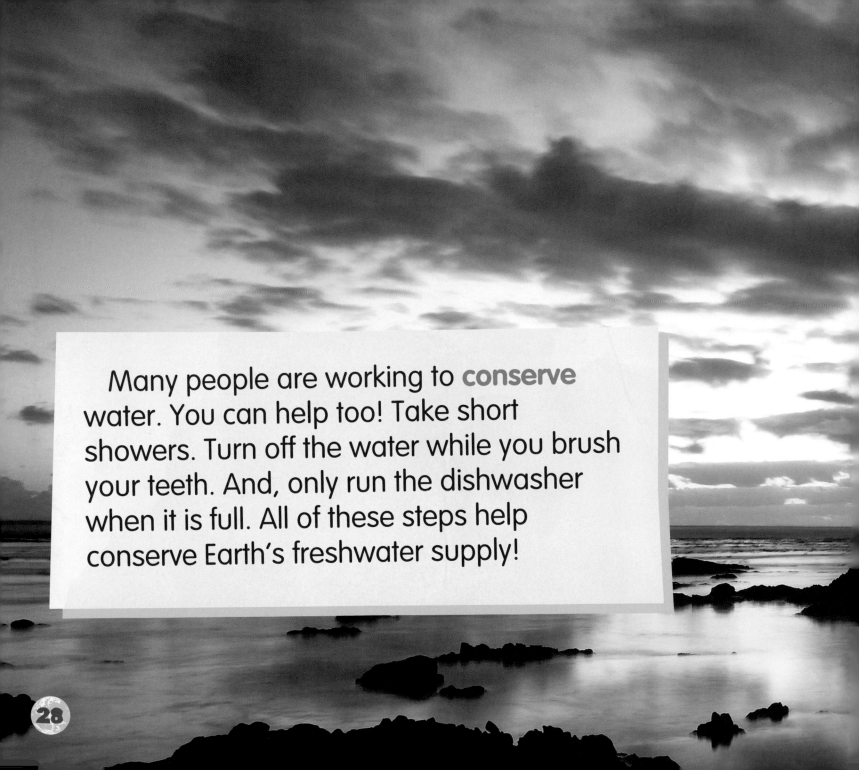

Many people are working to **conserve** water. You can help too! Take short showers. Turn off the water while you brush your teeth. And, only run the dishwasher when it is full. All of these steps help conserve Earth's freshwater supply!

Water is an important part of Earth's natural wonder!

DOWN TO EARTH:
A FEW MORE FACTS ABOUT THE WATER CYCLE

- Often, water in the water cycle stops moving. It stays in one form and location for a long time. This is true of much water found in **glaciers** (*right*), oceans, and aquifers.
- Plants let out water vapor. They draw up water from the ground through their roots. Then, they pass it out through their leaves as water vapor. This **process** is called transpiration.
- What if all the water in the **atmosphere** rained down at once? It would cover the ground about one inch (3 cm).

IMPORTANT WORDS

atmosphere (AT-muh-sfihr) the layer of gases that surrounds a planet.

conserve to avoid wasteful or harmful use of something.

formation something that has been formed into a shape.

glacier (GLAY-shuhr) a huge chunk of ice and snow on land.

process a natural order of actions.

seep to flow slowly through small openings.

shortage a lack in the amount needed.

WEB SITES

To learn more about the water cycle, visit ABDO Publishing Company online. Web sites about the water cycle are featured on our Book Links page. These links are routinely monitored and updated to provide the most current information available.

www.abdopublishing.com

INDEX

air **4, 14, 15, 16, 18, 22, 24, 30**

aquifers **12, 13, 26, 30**

Asia **11**

Baikal, Lake **11**

clouds **9, 18, 19, 20, 22**

condensation **8, 9, 18, 19, 20**

conservation **26, 27, 28**

dew **20, 21**

Earth **4, 5, 10, 11, 12, 14, 15, 20, 22, 25, 26, 28, 29**

evaporation **8, 9, 14, 15, 18, 24, 25**

fog **20, 21**

freshwater bodies **9, 10, 11, 13, 24**

glaciers **26, 30**

gravity **10**

Great Lakes **11**

humidity **16**

ice **6, 7, 9, 15**

infiltration **12**

land **4, 23, 24, 25**

oceans **4, 9, 10, 15, 24, 30**

precipitation **8, 9, 10, 22, 23, 24, 25, 30**

snow **6, 9, 10, 15, 22, 24**

sublimation **15**

transpiration **30**

United States **11**

water vapor **6, 7, 9, 14, 15, 16, 17, 18, 20, 21, 25, 30**